ON
ARCHITECTURE

A JOURNAL

■ ■

Front cover:
Shu-Xiang Xi
Kiosk, Smithsonian Institution, Washington, D.C., 1990
Elevation
Ink brush, 23 x 18 in.
Designed by Shepley, Bulfinch, Richardson & Abbott, Boston
Reproduced from *Architecture in Perspective V,*
The American Society of Architectural Perspectivists
© Shu-Xiang Xi

Published by Pomegranate Artbooks
Box 6099
Rohnert Park
California 94927

© 1994 Pomegranate Artbooks

ISBN 0-87654-085-X
Catalog No. A765

Pomegranate publishes several other illustrated journals as well as books, address books, calendars, notecards, posters, bookmarks and postcards. For information on our full range of publications, please write to Pomegranate, Box 6099, Rohnert Park, California 94927.

Designed by Bonnie Smetts Design
Printed in Korea

ON
.. ARCHITECTURE

It is unfortunate that architecture has come to be regarded as an intellectual enterprise understood only by a studied elite. It is not a required area of study in a general liberal arts education, and most students—except for learning the difference between Doric, Ionic and Corinthian columns—are not exposed to architecture unless they opt to take courses in it in college. Since it is not presented as a part of secondary school education, it has developed a mysterious and complicated reputation, seemingly beyond the judgment of those lacking the requisite graduate degrees.

The weighty shroud that surrounds architecture is not evident in other equally demanding artistic and professional disciplines. Most of us are quick to decide if a painting is good, determining in the first moment whether it draws us in or bores us or repels us. We do not hang a picture on our living room wall simply because we read somewhere that it is a good painting. We have to *like* it. The same is true of sculpture, of china, of glass, of textiles. Neither do we place our physical well-being in the hands of a doctor we deem incompetent, even though we lack an education in medicine. And without studying law, we know a good lawyer when we find one. But too many of us are hesitant to consider the esthetics of buildings, even though we are surrounded by them and live and work within them most of the time.

Of course, the truth is that we can love or hate a building without ever having designed one, just as we can love a painting without ever having held a brush, just as we can appreciate a Chopin piano concerto without ever having touched the keys. Architecture is more a part of our daily lives than any other art—changing the faces of our communities and defining the environments of all our different activities—and we therefore should take pause to notice each building we encounter.

Architectural renderings are beautifully effective, multifunctional tools for studying buildings. Whether intended as simple working plans or as more finished presentation drawings, the finest renderings help both builder and viewer realize the architect's intent. More importantly, these drawings symbolize the cultural values of their time. One need only contrast the drawings of, for example, Richard Morris Hunt (1827–1895) with those of Michael Graves (b. 1934) or Roger Dean (b. 1944) to grasp the true import of shared cultural norms in this most cultural of art forms.

The most successful and beautiful renderings almost always employ one of several methods of orthographic projection. These perspective drawings can present an entire building from various views so that it can be seen all at once, making a cathedral or a high-rise available for close scrutiny. They can lead us through the rooms of a country manor or up and down the stairs of an opera house in a minute. Such works of art are certainly worthy of a place on any number of museum walls, and they evoke the same depth of feeling as other fine drawings and paintings.

This journal contains drawings by such renowned architects as Hugh Ferriss, Frank Lloyd Wright, Charles Garnier, Michael Graves, Benjamin Henry Latrobe, Charles Moore, Buckminster Fuller and Richard Morris Hunt, among others. It includes the more fantastical work of Robert Mallet-Stevens, Roger Dean and Squire Vickers, as well as an abstract representation of New York skyscrapers painted by Joseph Stella and a fascinatingly impossible drawing by M. C. Escher. The deliberate variety of this selection intends to suggest that all structures of all sizes and shapes—existing buildings, those needing remodeling and those planned to be built—contribute to our environment and that imagination, beauty and efficiency must be considered if our urban, suburban and rural environments are to remain pleasing to us. As Karl Friedrich Schinkel wrote, "No object that has the quality of being solid, and of being formed and remodelled to fulfill a purpose, should be banished from architecture, for whatever can advantageously be used for creating structures contributes to the variety of architecture."

Hugh Ferriss AMERICAN, 1889–1962

Philosophy 1928

From the series created for *The Metropolis of Tomorrow*, published in 1929
Charcoal pencil on paper, 38 x 22 in.
© Avery Architectural and Fine Arts Library, Columbia University

*To portray the proposed
building is to portray
something that does not
exist; rendering is an
excercise in imagination….
It is a matter of equating
artistic reach with
architectural grasp.*

❖

HUGH FERRISS

*...a simple wave of a few
materials articulates space
into rooms...*

❖

RUDOLPH M. SCHINDLER

A house is a living machine.

❖

LE CORBUSIER

EAST FRONT FOR LENOX LIBRARY

Alexander Jackson Davis AMERICAN, 1803–1892
East front of Lenox Library on Fifth Avenue
between 70th and 71st Streets, New York, New York

Elevation and plan
Watercolor on paper, 14¼ x 10 in.
© Avery Architectural and Fine Arts Library, Columbia University

Architecture, the Queen of the fine arts,
assisted by her handmaids, Painting and
Sculpture, combines and displays all the
mighty powers of music and poetry. . . .
Hence arises that proud pre-eminence
which architecture by prescriptive right
seems to hold over the fine arts.

ALEXANDER JACKSON DAVIS

A standard form and a poetic form exist in any language or in any art.

❖

MICHAEL GRAVES

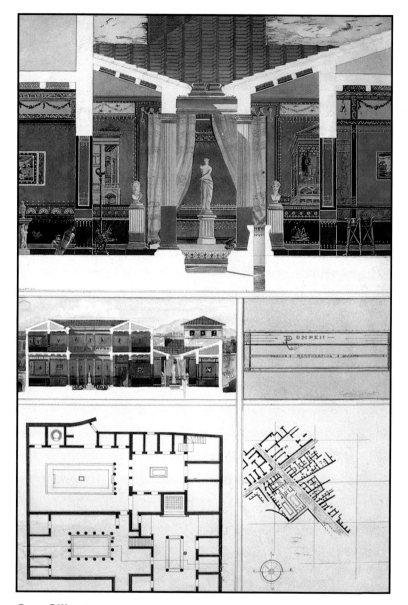

Cass Gilbert AMERICAN, 1859–1934

Restoration of Pompeii c. 1877

Painting and mathematics are as indispensable to the architect as the knowledge of metrical feet and syllables is to the poet, and I doubt whether a superficial knowledge of these arts will suffice.

❖

LEON BATTISTA ALBERTI

All animals, except man, adapt to their environment. Man changes his environment, making it adapt to him.

❖

R. BUCKMINSTER FULLER

M. C. Escher DUTCH, 1898–1972

Belvedere 1958

Lithograph, 18¼ x 11⅜ in.
© 1994 M. C. Escher/Cordon Art, Baarn, Holland

*My subjects are often so
playful. I can't keep from
fooling around with our
irrefutable certainties.*

M. C. ESCHER

*Architect: One who drafts
a plan of your house,
and plans a draft
of your money.*

❖

AMBROSE BIERCE

David Roberts SCOTTISH, 1796–1864

Grand Portico of the Temple of Philae, Nubia (DETAIL)

From the book *Views of Egypt and Nubia*, c. 1849
Lithograph
© The Huntington Library

*Since the beginnings
of cultural development,
the style of building has
always been the expression
of the disposition of and
the ability of the peoples
of all ages.*

❖

OTTO WAGNER

_Architects are a lot of
fools—always forgetting
that houses need staircases._

❖

GUSTAVE FLAUBERT

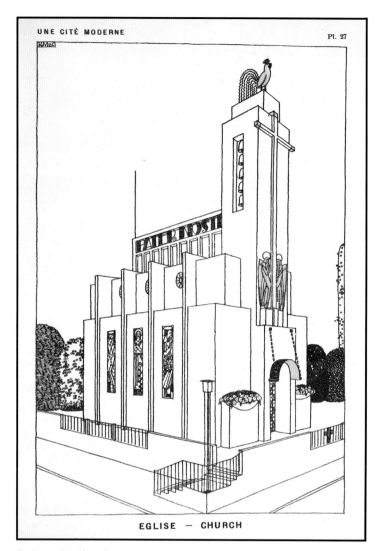

EGLISE — CHURCH

Robert Mallet Stevens FRENCH, 1886–1945
Church

Plate 27 from *A Modern City,* published in London in 1922 by Benn Brothers Ltd.
Prints and Photographs Division
Library of Congress

*[Architecture] embraces the
consideration of the whole
external surroundings of
the life of man; we cannot
escape from it if we would
…for it means the
moulding and altering to
human needs of the very
face of earth itself.*

❖

WILLIAM MORRIS

Benjamin Henry Latrobe AMERICAN, 1764–1820

John Harvie house RICHMOND, VIRGINIA (DETAIL)

Longitudinal and cross sections
Architecture, Design and Engineering Collections
Prints and Photographs Division, Library of Congress

*Architecture is my
delight…but it is an
enthusiasm of which I am
not ashamed, as its object
is to improve the taste of
my countrymen, to increase
their reputation, to
reconcile them to the rest of
the world and procure
them its praise.*

❖

THOMAS JEFFERSON

Architectural work must possess a spiritual content, provided, of course, that it completely fulfills the demands of appropriateness.

❖

LE CORBUSIER

Are you really sure
that a floor can't also
be a ceiling?
❖
M. C. ESCHER

Lying in bed would be altogether a perfect and supreme experience if only one had a coloured pencil long enough to draw on the ceiling.

❖

G. K. CHESTERTON

Charles Garnier

"Grand Escalier D'Honneur, Partie Superieure"

Plate 11–12 from *Le Nouvel Opera de Paris, Volume II*
Rare Book and Special Collections Division
Library of Congress

*I can imagine nothing
gloomier than a monument
consisting of a plane
surface, bare and
unadorned, made of a
light-absorbent material
absolutely stripped of detail,
its decoration consisting of
shadows outlined by still
deeper shadows.*

ETIENNE-LOUIS BOULEE

Eureka! (I've got it!)

❖

Attributed to
ARCHIMEDES

from *Vitruvius Pollio, De Architectura*

Roger Dean ENGLISH, B. 1944
Design for Sydney Harbour Development, International Pavilion 1983

© 1984 Roger Dean

*Buildings, I have insisted
for a long time, can and
must speak to us, which
requires that we grant
them freedom of speech, the
chance to say things that
are unimportant, even
silly, so when they are
grave or portentous we can
tell the difference.*

❖

CHARLES MOORE

Every work of architecture
is a work of cooperation.
❖
WILLIAM MORRIS

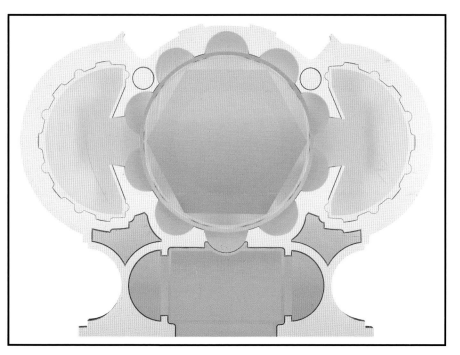

Thomas Akawie AMERICAN, B. 1935

Palladio Headboard 1967

Based on the plan for a Roman temple as described in a reconstruction drawing by Andrea Palladio (1508–1580);
in *The Fourth Book of Architecture,* plate XXIV, 1570
Acrylic on masonite, 48 x 66 in.
© Thomas Akawie

*That work therefore
cannot be called perfect,
which should be useful and
not durable, or durable
and not useful, or having
both these should be
without beauty.*

ANDREA PALLADIO

He builded better than he knew;
The conscious stone to beauty grew.

❖

RALPH WALDO EMERSON

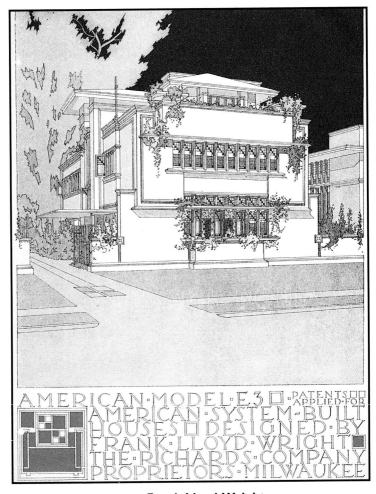

AMERICAN·MODEL·E3 □ ·PATENTS□□ ·APPLIED·FOR
AMERICAN·SYSTEM-BUILT
HOUSES □ DESIGNED·BY
FRANK·LLOYD·WRIGHT■
THE·RICHARDS·COMPANY
PROPRIETORS·MILWAUKEE

Frank Lloyd Wright AMERICAN, 1867–1959

American Model E3

Perspective
One of a series of American System-Built Houses designed for The Richards Company, Milwaukee, Wisconsin
Architecture, Design and Engineering Collections
Library of Congress

*A rational, important
change in civilization is
possible because
architecture for the
individual becomes not
only reasonable but is the
only possible architecture.
So the architecture of
democracy is here.*

FRANK LLOYD WRIGHT

*I am and always will be
an unrepentent visualist.*

❖

LE CORBUSIER

Joseph Stella AMERICAN, B. ITALY, 1877–1946

The Skyscrapers 1920–1922

Panel 3 of *The Voice of the City of New York Interpreted*
Oil and tempera on canvas, 99¾ x 54 in.
Collection of The Newark Museum
Purchase 1937, Felix Fuld Bequest Fund
© The Newark Museum

*New York is a tribute to
the Beaux-Arts so far as
surface decoration goes,
and underneath a tribute
to the American engineer.*

FRANK LLOYD WRIGHT

*Invention often occurs
when individuals,
frustrated by circumstances,
try to transform their
environment rather than to
reform human nature.*

❖

R. BUCKMINSTER FULLER

MONOHEX "FLY'S EYE" GEODESIC STRUCTURES

Buckminster Fuller AMERICAN, 1895–1983

Geodesic Structures—Monohex

Drawings filed with United States Patent Office, 1961
© Buckminster Fuller Institute

I live on Earth at present, and I don't know what I am.
I know that I am not a category. I am not a thing—a noun.
I seem to be a verb, an evolutionary process—
an integral function of the universe.

❖

R. BUCKMINSTER FULLER

It is in perfect regularity
that the beauty
of form lies.

❖

ETIENNE-LOUIS BOULEE

_____

_____

_____

_____

_____

_____

_____

_____

_____

_____

_____

_____

_____

_____

_____

_____

_____

_____

_____

_____

_____

_____

Squire Vickers AMERICAN, 1872–1947
Fantasy Castle with Men on Zebras 1923

Oil on panel, 34⅝ x 26¼ in.
© Estate of Ruth A. Vickers,
courtesy Shepherd Gallery, New York

*[The architect] feels the
most profound destiny of
the building immediately
in his own being.
Only at this point does the
question arise: what are
the means necessary to
realize such an idea
produced in total freedom?*
❖
KARL FRIEDRICH SCHINKEL

Let your watchword
be order,
your beacon beauty.
❖
BERNARD MAYBECK

RESIDENCE FOR A. STERN, ESQ.ᴿᴱ SAN FRANCISCO, CAL. RICHARD HOWLAND HVNT, ARCH'T.

SCALE 3/8 INCH = ONE FOOT

Richard Howland Hunt AMERICAN, 1862–1931

Residence of A. Stern, San Francisco, California c. 1899–1903

When we mean to build,
We first survey the plot, then draw the model;
And when we see the figure of the house,
Then we must rate the cost of the erection;
Which if we find outweighs ability,
What do we do then but draw anew the model
In fewer offices, or at last desist
To build at all?

❖

WILLIAM SHAKESPEARE, *Henry IV, Part 2*

Front elevation, presentation drawing
Pencil, ink and watercolor on paper on mounting board
The Prints and Drawings Collection
of The Octagon Museum
of The American Architectural Foundation
© The American Architectural Foundation

Light, God's eldest daughter, is a principal beauty in a building.

❖

THOMAS FULLER

Charles Rennie Mackintosh SCOTTISH, 1868–1928

Drawing Room Fireplace (above)
and Music Room Piano (below)

Elevations
From *House for an Art Lover*, 1901
Glasgow School of Art
© GSA Enterprises, Ltd., Glasgow, Scotland

Architecture is the world of
art, and as it is everything
visible and invisible that
makes the world,
so it is all the arts and
crafts and industries that
make architecture.

❖

CHARLES RENNIE MACKINTOSH

*Modern architecture starts
with Mackintosh in
Scotland, Otto Wagner
in Vienna and
Louis Sullivan in Chicago.*
❖

RUDOLPH M. SCHINDLER

RAJA TAGORE · RESIDENCE · CALCUTTA
WALTER BURLEY GRIFFIN · ARCHITECT ·

Walter Burley Griffin AMERICAN, 1876–1937

Raja Tagore residence, Calcutta, India c. 1936

*The real architect will
expend the same energy on
a woodcutter's house as he
would on the greatest
commission.*

❖

CLAUDE-NICOLAS LEDOUX

No really Italian building
seems ill at ease in Italy.

❖

FRANK LLOYD WRIGHT

Richard Morris Hunt 1827–1895

Theatre for a Small City (DETAIL) 1851

Section
École des Beaux-Arts, Projet Rendu
Ink and watercolor on paper
The Prints and Drawings Collection of The Octagon Museum
of The American Architectural Foundation
© The American Architectural Foundation

*Once aware of and
responsive to the possible
cultural influences on
building, it is important
that society's patterns of
ritual be registered
in the architecture.*

❖

MICHAEL GRAVES

*Nothing can be allowed
in good architecture for
the introduction of which
a good reason cannot
be assigned.*

❖

SIR JOHN SLOANE

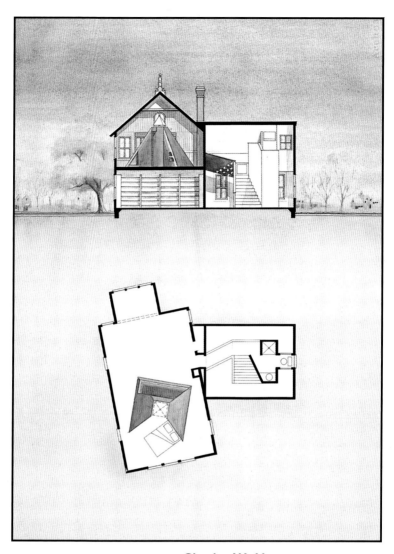

Charles W. Moore AMERICAN, B. 1925

Moore House, Renovation, Essex, Connecticut 1970–1975

Plan and section
Ink and watercolor on paper, 30 x 22½ in.
Drawing by Robert Shemwell
© Charles W. Moore

*To find an original man
living in an original house,
is as satisfactory as to find
an eagle's nest built on top
of a mountain crag.*

ANDREW JACKSON DOWNING

The history of art is the history of revivals.

❖

SAMUEL BUTLER

Sany Building
Tokyo

Michael Graves AMERICAN, B. 1934
The SANY Building TOKYO, JAPAN 1991

Kanda River elevation
© Graves Design

In its rejection
of the human or
anthropomorphic
representation of previous
architecture, the Modern
Movement undermined
the poetic form in favor of
nonfigural, abstract
geometries.

❖

MICHAEL GRAVES

The physician can bury his mistakes, but the architect can only advise his client to plant vines.

❖

FRANK LLOYD WRIGHT

Adolfo Carlos Muñoz del Monte D. 1899

Country House for a Dramatist 1886

Design problem for the School of Architecture, Columbia University
© Avery Architectural and Fine Arts Library, Columbia University

*In every architectural order
only the column, the
entablature and the
pediment could form an
essential part of its
composition. If each of
these three parts is suitably
placed and suitably formed,
nothing else need be added
to make the work perfect.*

❖

ABBÉ LAUGIER

*The rendering is a means
toward an end;
the end is architecture.*

❖

HUGH FERRISS

Shu-Xiang Xi

Kiosk, Smithsonian Institution, Washington, D.C. 1990

Elevation
Ink brush, 23 x 18 in.
Designed by Shepley, Bulfinch, Richardson & Abbott, Boston
Reproduced from *Architecture in Perspective V,*
The American Society of Architectural Perspectivists
© Shu-Xiang Xi

*Since mankind has been
aware of the greatness of
classical antiquity, the
great architects have been
bound by one idea. They
have thought: The ancient
Romans would have solved
this task in the same way
as I do today, if they had
been in my position.*

❖

ADOLF LOOS

There is the architect, up among the whirlwinds and clouds that battle to dominate the skies.

❖

CLAUDE-NICOLAS LEDOUX

James B. McBurney
New Ukranian Orthodox Church 1990

Watercolor, pencil and ink, 19 x 21 in.
Designed by Frank D. Nemeth
Reproduced from *Architecture in Perspective V,*
The American Society of Architectural Perspectivists
© James B. McBurney

*The ultimate aim of all
visual arts is the complete
building…. Together let us
desire, conceive and create
the new structure of the
future, which will embrace
architecture and sculpture
and painting in one unity
and which will one day
rise toward heaven from
the hands of a million
workers like the crystal
symbol of a new faith.*

❖

WALTER GROPIUS

Vanity and stupidity will overcome mountains. The landowner must flourish his purse; the architect lacks conviction.

❖

RUDOLPH M. SCHINDLER

Richard Morris Hunt 1827–1895

Residence of Frederic E. Church OLANA, NEW YORK

Front elevation, c. 1867
Pencil, ink and watercolor on French blue paper
The Prints and Drawings Collection of The Octagon Museum of The American Architectural Foundation
© The American Architectural Foundation

*I consider this triumph of
Realism to be favorable to
art, since I am of the
opinion that enough tasks
will offer themselves to the
architect's better half, the
artist, which will require
all his talent and skill for
their solution.*

OTTO WAGNER

_____

_____

_____

_____

_____

_____

_____

_____

_____

_____

_____

_____

_____

_____

_____

_____

_____

_____

_____

_____

_____

_____

We make buildings for our need, and then, sacrificing our pockets to art, cover them with a mass of purely nonsensical forms which we hope may turn them into fine architecture.

❖

ROGER FRY

Hugh Ferriss AMERICAN, 1889–1962

"Fallingwater," house for Edgar Kaufmann BEAR RUN, PENNSYLVANIA

Charcoal on paper mounted on board, 8½ x 13¼ in.
Designed by Frank Lloyd Wright
Published in *Power in Buildings,* 1953
© Avery Architectural and Fine Arts Library, Columbia University

I have already mentioned
an indefinable element
that makes some builders
"master builders."
During a day-long
contemplation of Taliesin,
that isolated work of art in
the desert, it seemed likely
that this element is love.

HUGH FERRISS

What diversity, when the
rising sun spreads its
shadow over the earth!
What flickering effects
when the moon traces
labyrinths of light
on the building!

❖

CLAUDE-NICOLAS LEDOUX

Thomas Ustick Walter AMERICAN, 1804–1887

United States Capitol, Library of Congress, Second Gallery Doors

Architectural drawing showing details in plans, elevations and sections, 1862
Graphite, ink and watercolor
Architecture, Design and Engineering Collections
Prints and Photographs Division
Library of Congress

[Studying philosophy]
makes an architect
high-minded and not
self-assuming, but rather
renders him courteous,
just, and honest without
avariciousness.

VITRUVIUS

*Whatever the character
of the thinking,
just so was the character
of the building.*

❖

LOUIS SULLIVAN

Cass Gilbert AMERICAN, 1859–1934
The Duomo in Florence, Italy

The Cupola of San Maria del Fiore Cathedral, 1417–1454
Watercolor architectural rendering
Designed by Filippo Brunelleschi (1377–1446)
Architecture, Design and Engineering Collections
Prints and Photographs Division
Library of Congress

Architecture cannot lie,
and buildings, although
inanimate, are to
that extent morally
superior to men.

❖

JOHN GLOAG

[Would you prefer] a white house resembling a bird that has just dropped down on your hilltop, or an earth-colored one that seems to rise out of it?

❖

BERNARD MAYBECK

Tainer Associates Ltd. Rendering Group, Chicago

Villa Quadrata PROSPECT HEIGHTS, ILLINOIS

Airbrush, marker and paint, 26 x 26 in.
Designed by Tainer Associates Ltd.
Reproduced from *Architecture in Perspective V*,
The American Society of Architectural Perspectivists
© Tainer Associates Ltd.

*No object that has the quality of being solid, and
of being formed and remodeled to fulfill a purpose,
should be banished from architecture, for
whatever can advantageously be used for creating
structures contributes to the variety of architecture.*

❖

KARL FRIEDRICH SCHINKEL